LIVELY
MAY I WALK

"Wandering on paths of beauty,
  Lively may I walk."

—Navajo Indian night chant

LIVELY
MAY I WALK

Devotions for the Golden Years

GLENN H. ASQUITH

ABINGDON PRESS

NEW YORK   NASHVILLE

LIVELY MAY I WALK

Copyright © 1960 by Abingdon Press

Library of Congress Catalog Card Number: 60-9193

SET UP, PRINTED, AND BOUND BY THE
PARTHENON PRESS, AT NASHVILLE,
TENNESSEE, UNITED STATES OF AMERICA

Lovingly dedicated to my parents
GEORGE AND MARY ASQUITH

Preface

There are rich treasures in life.

There are the treasures of the years past carefully stored away in memory and record.

There are the treasures of the present as we look around us at the marvels of the world in our time, and as we mingle with others who cross our path.

And, best of all, there are the treasures of the years and the life to come.

But often these treasures are stored in hidden caves as was the treasure of Ali Baba, and they may be seen and enjoyed only by those who know the Sesame to open the doors.

The following pages hold suggestions to help you find your magic word with which to throw back the curtains and the gates between you and the wonderful treasure which God has for you.

And, as Russell Conwell brought out in his lecture, "The Acre of Diamonds," the treasure will be found in your own backyard, off the bow of your ship of life, in your own mind and soul.

GLENN H. ASQUITH

Contents

9

CONTENTS

1. THE BEST OF VISION

"For now we see through a glass, darkly; but then face to face."   —I Cor. 13:12

"Wait until I clean your windshield," requests the attendant at the gasoline station.

Impatient to be on his way, the driver of the car mutters, "Don't bother."

But when the job is done, the traveler marvels, "I did not know it was so dirty."

Walking the roads of our days, life splashes and splotches our spiritual vision. Worries, troubles, illnesses, disappointments leave their obscuring marks. Added to this, we develop our own peculiarities and prejudices which cover the inner sight like a pair of dark glasses. Everything must come through to us tinged by our willfulness.

And, as though this were not enough, each of us has inherited some errors from the past. Just as nearsightedness, farsightedness and astigmatism distort physical seeing, so do traits slant inner seeing. We are of a certain nation. We are of a certain race. We are of a certain class. We are masculine or feminine. From each grouping we take an individual way of looking at things.

Always through a glass, or always through the medium of a mirror, we peer heavenward. Is it any wonder that we are not content with the view? Shall we be free of the glass—ever? Yes, and yes, and yes!

The glass is for *now*, perfect vision is for *then*. *Now* is wrapped upon us in layers. Each day removes a layer, and each day brings better vision. Hourly, we are given a nearer view of the face of our heavenly Father.

Meditate a moment, and then read Joel 2:28-32.

Prayer: Cleanse my vision, O Lord, open my eyes, free me from the glass of my imperfections. AMEN.

2. THE BEST OF LIGHT

"But it shall be one day which shall be known to the Lord, not day nor night: but it shall come to pass, that at evening time it shall be light."—Zech. 14:7

There is no light switch which can turn off the sun. And the sun never sets, but constantly, continually, the sun shines. Why then do we have daylight and darkness? Why do we have dawn, morning, noon, afternoon, evening, night?

The answer is that our world does not hold still. The great light of the sun is always available, but our world insists on moving. It turns every twenty-four hours, and it moves around the sun every year.

What is true of the natural light of the sun is true of the light of God. John described this light when he spoke of Jesus as "the true light, which lighteth every man that cometh into the world." This light of God never fails, is never withdrawn. Why then do we have times of despair, of unbelief, of bitter tears, of sighing for the past?

Here again the answer is that our inner world will not hold still. Each of us has his own private world made up of many interests. There are work, family, friends, hobbies, ambitions, the physical body. And this world of our daily activities and concerns turns us away from God all too frequently.

Unhappily we become so accustomed to being borne away from our Savior by our private world that we grow to *expect* life will have midnights.

God has planned something wonderful for us—a day that is to be known to him and by him as a special day. This special day will have no growing dusk, it will be marked by an increase of light, and it will know no lingering shadows. Marvel of marvels! At evening time by our earthly watches the light will come to its perfect, glowing fullness.

We can think that the prophet who brought us our text must have had human life in mind. A day begins with dawn and ends at sunset? A life begins at birth and ends in death? This is true with men, but not with God.

With God it is always endless day, because his is the light that never fails. With God a life is brighter and nearer his perfect light as the years go by.

Continue the thought by reading Rom. 8:18-28.

Prayer: Grant, my Father, that I may cease turning away from thee until I bask ever in the light of thy love. AMEN.

3. THE BEST OF LAUGHTER

"Then was our mouth filled with laughter, and our tongue with singing: then said they among the heathen, The Lord hath done great things for them."

—Ps. 126:2

"He who laughs last, laughs best." Is not this the old saying which our fathers and mothers taught us? But what does it mean?

We laughed in childhood, but now we cannot remember why. Just to see a kitten frisking, or perhaps because someone made a funny face. Or maybe it was because we were invited to a party.

We laughed in our youth, but now we cannot remember why. Perhaps it was because we hit or caught a ball. We were glad school was out. We first felt the boy-girl tug in the heart.

We laughed in the strength of manhood and womanhood, but now we cannot remember why. The bills were all paid for once. A new baby had come to the house. A vacation was planned.

The laughter of the past is all so vague now and some of it seems rather silly.

But now is the time for the best laughter. Can we laugh now, in our maturity?

The lines of a hymn come back:

> Count your many blessings,
> See what God hath done.

Oh, the things which the Lord hath done for us!

Here we are, and we look back upon sunshine and starlight, hard work and play, and blessed sleep. We recognize love and friendship and dear faces. We see things that have been accomplished and are now done with.

Here we are, and we look around. The same wonderful world filled with wonderful people, books and music, and the doings of the world.

Here we are, and we look ahead. The tranquillity and poise which the years have brought. All this— and then heaven too.

At the last we laugh, and we know why. We are the beloved children of God.

For more of this, see Job 8:19-22.

Prayer: For joy I thank thee Lord. For the laughter of peace and hope, I praise thee. AMEN.

4. THE BEST OF FRIENDS

"Go home to thy friends, and tell them how great things the Lord hath done for thee."—Mark 5:19

"But this bill is too large! There must be a mistake. See, I am crossing through the amount and I shall put down just half of that sum." So spoke the steward in the parable.

This man knew he was about to lose his job because of his wrongdoing, and he said to himself that he would be kind to the men who owed his employer money so that they would take him into their houses if he was put out of work. He made friends for himself along the way.

In a way we do the same in life. As we work and struggle to keep going, we take time to make friends. By constant use, the Bible becomes a friend. Our church becomes a friend. A few good books become part of us. Some music weaves itself into our souls. A hobby will be a friend for idle hours. Thoughts and habits treated kindly will remain friends. A small group of men and women, young people, children are our comfort. The eternal God is closer than breathing, nearer than hand or foot.

In the hurry of life we see so little of these friends.

But as time goes on we hear the blessed instruction, "Go home to thy friends." And we will find that they will take us in. We have been kind to them through the years. And in proportion as we have chosen our friends wisely will our joy abound. As we have been careful to select worthy companions will be our welcome.

It is the same as a traveler going wearily from land to land buying beautiful things in each country and shipping them to his home. Finally, his wanderings over, he himself goes home and finds his treasures—his friends—awaiting him. For the rest of his life he has fellowship with the things he has loved.

Another glimpse of this in Luke 15.

Prayer: O Lord, may the best of my life, especially thy love, be my joy in these days. AMEN.

5. THE BEST OF LOVE

"Greater love hath no man than this, that a man lay down his life for his friends." —John 15:13

In our school books there was a fascinating picture of Sir Walter Raleigh taking off his coat. He spread this garment across a mud puddle in order that his Queen might cross the puddle without staining her garments.

Day by day, hour by hour, we lay down our lives. There are bad spots in the world, and we would save others from harm. Mothers lay down their lives minute by minute for their children. Fathers by toiling lay down their lives for their families. Grocers spend their lives to feed people. In factories the workers give their lives to make needful products. Any worthy task in the home or out of it calls for life giving for others.

Behind all of this is love. Yes, the greatest and best of love. When the time comes that there is not much life left to give, love floods in. From every spot where we have left a moment or a day as a bridge for others comes love. Life is never given in vain.

The best of these days is the turning to the

Saviour. We find that we have something in common with him. Jesus gave his life for us all. His life became the bridge from earth to heaven. His life filled the void between man and the Creator. His life, laid across the morass of sin, united man and God. If he has failed, we have failed. If he has succeeded, we have succeeded. We have tried earnestly to follow his example. His was the greatest work of all ages. Our work is small in comparison, but the same kind of love was in his heart and ours.

Without pride or boasting, we may look back to where we left our life for the sake of someone in need, and receive it back tenfold.

Read again I Cor. 13.

Prayer: I thank thee, Lord, for showing me how to give away my life in order to save it. AMEN.

6. THE BEST OF MYSTERY

"But we speak the wisdom of God in a mystery, even the hidden wisdom, which God ordained before the world unto our glory." —I Cor. 2:7

Before Christmas Day, who enjoys peeking into the packages to ferret out and ruin the surprises?

And yet we ask:

Why *does* God . . . ?

Why *doesn't* God . . . ?

Why does God permit the taking of a young person of great usefulness in the world? Why does God permit the idle lingering of the aged whose work seems to be done? Why is pain? Why doesn't God step in and order peace in the world? Why are children ungrateful to parents? Why does hard work apparently go unrewarded? Oh, a thousand "Whys" and "Why-nots" as the days go on!

There are many mysteries in God's way with us. Many things are beyond our limited ability to know. But this we are promised—all will be to our final glory.

A child lives in a child's world mentally and physically, but he enjoys and uses the products of adult minds and efforts. We live in a physical world while enjoying the riches of the spiritual. Some things of the eternal are brought down to our level of understanding—other things remain beyond our reach.

If the small surprises and mysteries of the day are precious and exciting—God's wonders to be revealed must be magnificent!

Puzzling over one of his favorite mysteries, an aged professor said that the first moment he was in heaven he was going to hunt up the apostle Paul and ask, "Who wrote the book of Hebrews?" Each of us has questions to be answered which make the future exciting even beyond the other glories to be revealed.

The thought may be continued by reading Job 38.

Turning to God: Heavenly Father, make me truly grateful for the glorious things I have come to know in life. Make me even more grateful for the mysteries which shall be revealed. Today may I understand more than I did yesterday. AMEN.

7. THE BEST OF SELF

"The Lord Jesus Christ . . . shall change our vile body, that it may be fashioned like unto his glorious body." —Phil. 3:20, 21

What is left? . . .

Youth has come to an end—what is left? Faculties of the body are not so keen—what is left? The daily work is about done—what is left? Early ambitions and passions move us no more—what is left? Why, the best is left!

As it was one day in a sculptor's studio: Michelangelo was pounding away at a beautiful piece of marble and each blow of his hammer on the chisel sent chips of stone flying. An intelligent, sensitive woman came to visit, and was horrified to see what her artist friend was doing to the lovely marble block. Picking up a chip from the floor she held it out toward the master, in tearful reproach. But he replied:

> With chiselled touch
> The stone unhewn and cold
> Becomes a living mold,
> The more the marble wastes
> The more the statue grows.[1]

[1] Translated by Mrs. Henry Roscoe.

There are the chips of years lying around us. There are the chips of memories of good things past—of good friends gone. Shall we cry over the chips? Or shall we rejoice at the handiwork of our Master as he makes us more like himself? The more this outward form wastes, the more the inner likeness grows.

Each year leaves less of the chipping to be endured, and reveals more of the person that God intends to create—the person designed to occupy an eternal habitation.

The idea may be pursued by reading Heb. 12:1-11.

Prayer is the soul's sincere desire: O thou perfect One—holy, holy, holy, high and lifted up. I remember that I have been commanded to be perfect also. Help me to bear the poundings of fate. Give me patience under the gouging chisel of time. Make me to know that I am becoming more like the Master. AMEN.

8. THE BEST OF INDIVIDUALITY

"But every man hath his proper gift of God, one after this manner, and another after that."

—I Cor. 7:7b

We talk about the "big" people in the world . . . the famous, the great, the known; and the "little" people in the world . . . the obscure, the plodders, those who never get anywhere. God does not recognize such distinctions.

In the state of California we find two things to ponder over. There are some desert plants so tiny that a botanist must study them while lying flat on the ground. He must use a strong magnifying glass to see the various parts. Not many miles away are the giant redwood trees. Some are so huge that roadways have been cut through their trunks. And yet it has been proved that the tiny desert plant is just as perfect in its way as is the enormous tree. Each is doing in the world what God intended. Neither could do the work of the other.

More than this—among the tiny plants no two are alike, among the redwoods no two are alike. When billions of snowflakes fall during a winter storm the microscope can find no two identical. No two fingerprints are the same.

What a thought! There *is* no one, *has been* no one, and *will be* no one exactly like me. With God, I am a valuable collector's item!

Why talk, then, about small or little people? Size does not make a difference. Worldly importance is of no eternal importance. Even in obscurity and limitation one made in the image of God can be as perfect in usefulness and effort as a "great" man or woman. Small tools can fit in delicate places where large tools would be worse than useless. God needs the "still, small voice" more often than he needs the earthquake, wind, or fire.

Keep after this idea by reading Eph. 1:1-12.

A word to God: My Father, if the world has placed a low value on me—if I have failed according to my standards—when the shadows seem to overwhelm the light—remind me of the labor and love which thou hast expended to make me as I am. AMEN.

9. THE BEST OF TOMORROW

"But as it is written, Eye hath not seen, nor ear heard, neither have entered into the heart of man, the things which God hath prepared for them that love him."

—I Cor. 2:9

How wonderful is a curtain!

As we come to sit in an auditorium to enjoy a play, a concert, some other presentation, the curtain across the stage is enticing. What is behind that curtain? What do those mysterious sounds and rustlings mean? And how terrible to be late and miss that magic moment when the huge drape lifts—oh, so slowly!—to show us what was hidden behind.

And yet, even though we know this, we wonder why God does not tell us all that is to happen to us here and hereafter.

"If only I had known," we say, or "If only I knew."

But how drab a life that would be! Instead, God confronts us with magic curtains every day, and he gives us the joy of wondering. We wonder what it will be like to be forty—fifty—sixty—seventy—eighty? We wonder what the postman will bring. We wonder even about the weather.

And best of all we wonder as did Paul in his squalid prison cell in Rome. As he sat before the great curtain of his life, he wondered: "To live is Christ, but to die is great gain . . . now I see through a glass darkly, but then I shall know."

In any event, how could the Lord make us to know the things of tomorrow? We have only the eyes, ears, and hearts perceptive to what is familiar. And that which is to be in us and for us cannot be grasped by earthly faculties.

Is God cruel then to keep from us that which is to be, or is he, as always, most wonderfully kind? Each day—each moment—we set sail under sealed orders. New directions, new purposes, new adventures, new companions, new tasks which are kept secret until the last minute are far more exciting than to know that we have been placed in bondage to one situation for the rest of our lives.

Exploring this, read the entire chapter of I Cor. 2.

And thank God: Father of lights, in whom there is no shadow cast by turning: I thank thee for keeping the best in store; I thank thee for sending the Lord ahead to make a place ready for me. AMEN.

10. THE BEST OF PRAYER

"But when ye pray, use not vain repetitions, as the heathen do: for they think that they shall be heard for their much speaking." —Matt. 6:7

"And where have you been?" a sister asked of her brother.

They were on a luxurious ocean liner sailing for Europe. Daily the young woman had been on deck enjoying the sea and air. Daily she had made friends of fellow travelers. Daily she had taken the best from this happy experience. But her brother—! The brother disappeared after breakfast and was seldom seen until dinner. Now he stood before her disheveled, and a trifle sooty.

"Why, I have been down in the engine room helping around. I have to know what makes the ship run."

Their parents had given them this trip for a graduation present. The young man had no need to worry about the crew's duties. His first-class fare had been paid.

And are not our prayers like this? So often we ask for the bread-and-butter things. So often we are worried and concerned only for the things which keep life's ship moving. Let us say that we spend our time in the engine room of life. We worry over the grimy, everyday details.

But God has paid our passage. He knows about the engine room and the essential fuel; he knows about wind and tide. And yet he tells us to "seek first the kingdom" and then all these minor things will be added.

As in the world, so in the soul. We may ask for sunrise and sunset, or we may sit at the feet of Jesus as did Mary. We may ask and ask and ask, "Give me—give me—give me," seeking the things which perish. Have we forgotten that we are the heirs of God?

Words regarding such things may be found in Matt. 6:24-34.

A *beginning:* "Loving and good heavenly Father: time is short and prayer time is limited. Save me from wasting precious moments in vain recitals of bodily needs. Let my prayers be for high and holy things. AMEN.

11. THE BEST OF DISCIPLINE

"Blessed is the man whom thou chasteneth, O Lord, and teachest him out of thy law." —Ps. 94:12

In every great work of music there is a theme. Many of us would speak of it as the tune or melody. The theme is the real message of the symphony. And yet:

As the musicians play on and on the great clashing of drums and cymbals confuse us. We get lost when the horns sound loud and long. We think the theme is lost. But if we listen patiently we will find the melody again. And at the end it will come out triumphantly.

So does my life and yours have the purpose of God running through it. Trouble seems to break that purpose. Sorrow and bereavement cause us to feel that all is lost. Suffering and fear seem to nullify the purpose. But at the end, if we have faith, God's will is done in us triumphantly.

So it is with a piece of silver. The silversmith hammers cruelly; his instruments scrape and chase the soft metal. It seems as though the original design is lost forever, but at the last the piece is done and is worthy in beauty and grace to take an honored place in the world.

The Roman writer Epictetus told his pupils that a sea captain becomes skillful in proportion to the storms he goes through. Anyone can get along when the sailing is smooth, but the smooth water sailor would be lost in a tempest.

It is entirely possible that the one who numbers the most storms in his life has received the most from God. Have we not noticed how much stronger and more vigorous is the tree exposed to the winds and rains and snow than the one protected by a building or another tree? Who would choose to be a spiritual weakling?

For the promise read Rom. 8:26-39.

And be humble: My Lord, forbid that I should repine. Keep me from complaining. Help me to realize the promise that on the third day I shall be perfected. AMEN.

12. THE BEST OF INVESTMENTS

*"For where your treasure is, there will your heart
be also."*   —Luke 12:34

It had been a wonderful parade, and how the
children had enjoyed it!

But now the procession was over, and the boys and
girls who had spent their money for balloons were
brokenhearted. The balloons had burst and nothing was left but some sticky rubber on the sticks.

In a sense, life is a parade. And when we come
nearer to the end than the beginning, we shall have
spent our moments and our days for something.
Shall we end up with nothing but some sorry re-
mains of no value?

Sometimes we envy the one who has invested his
money wisely in bonds. We watch as he snips off
the coupons at intervals and exchanges them for
money again.

That is good—but there are better bonds. Perhaps we have invested our money in a young person's education—we shall be cashing dividends as
long as that man or woman serves humanity. Perhaps we have invested some time in church work
—we shall receive dividends both now and in eternal

life. Perhaps our love has been given freely to the needy, the discouraged, the lonely. We may expect returns forever. Perhaps a dream of our own has been left unfollowed in order that someone else might realize his dream. The losing of life will give us life.

Undoubtedly all of us have made some balloon investments. Why waste good time regretting them? We have so many good investments and our hearts are with them. Let us reap to the full our dividends of content and happiness. The treasure will be awaiting us at another turn in the road. The substance put into worldly things and selfish things will be as the purchase of wildcat mining stocks; and the substance and life we have given freely to God and man will prove to be "gilt-edged" and safe forever.

After meditation look up Matt. 16:24-28.

And pray: O Lord of eternal life, give me the vision to see how much joy is stored within my soul. Help me to taste of it. AMEN.

13. THE BEST OF ABUNDANCE

"And Elijah said unto Ahab, Get thee up, eat and drink; for there is a sound of abundance of rain."

—I Kings 18:41

James Martineau was a frail young man. Indeed, his concerned friends said, "If he lives to be thirty, it will be a miracle." But at the age of eighty-five Martineau wrote his greatest book.

And there was John Wesley. At fifty, Wesley spoke of himself as an old, worn-out man. But as he approached his ninetieth year this man of God was preaching with vigor and saving power.

What happened to these two men? There had come to them an abundance of life and vision. Jesus had this in mind when he said he had come that men might have life abundantly.

Perhaps we need to ask ourselves—what is an abundance? If we are talking of rain, the farmer will say that an abundance is not too little and not too much—but just enough. Too little will keep the crops sparse; too much will wash them out. Could we not say that the widow's oil and meal were in abundance? After all, when she tipped the oil jar enough came out for one day's supply, and when she dipped into the meal there was enough to go with the oil. When we pray, "Give us this day our daily bread," are we not asking for abundance?

The poet Keats, who died at the age of twenty-six, dreaded dying before his time.

> When I have fears that I may cease to be
> Before my pen has glean'd my teeming brain

He thought his weak body had not abundance to match his mind. But in his brief life he produced more of beauty than we have used.

Surely we have abundance of time. We have abundance of strength. We have abundance of all needful to accomplish our purpose in the world. Our Heavenly Father holds the wealth of all creation in his keeping, and he has loved us far beyond our understanding. How can we doubt that, with our Lord, he will freely give us all things in abundance?

For the whole story, I Kings 18:41-46.

Our prayer: Lord of the rain and the harvest, send an abundance. I do not ask for too much—but just enough. AMEN.

14. THE BEST OF COURAGE

"Be of good courage, and he shall strengthen your heart, all ye that hope in the Lord." —Ps. 31:24

At the Battle of Bunker Hill the bullets were thick, carrying death. The bayonets were cruelly sharp. There one of our captains named Callendar was proved a coward and General Washington took his rank from him and discharged him. But Callendar re-enlisted as a private and in a later battle he proved his courage, and he was made a captain once again.

What was the best of his courage? That he faced the foe without running? Or that he went back and tried again? Is not the real courage to go back and try again? Apparently the psalmist sensed the weakness of his own heart, and the weakness of the hearts of his fellows. He pointed out that God would give strong hearts to those with courage.

Our battle with a bad habit may have been lost. But a battle is not the whole war. Courage will send us back to try again. Our battle with despondency may have been lost. Courage can yet win the day and the prize of hope.

There are numerous daily battles: with impatience, with lack of faith, with hard-to-get-along-with companions, with fear, with pain, with waiting.

It is not cowardice to lose a battle now and then. Cowardice is to give up. It is said that Thomas Edison lost fifteen hundred battles in his attempt to make an electric light bulb, but he tried again and at last illuminated the world.

It matters, of course, who is on our side. God is on *our* side. So—who can be against us? Back we go, and this time to win!

A help: Deut. 31:1-8.

Talking to our Ally: O Lord who helped Joshua, who strengthened Jesus, who watched over Paul, strengthen and help and watch over me. AMEN.

15. THE BEST OF BEAUTY

"To appoint unto them that mourn in Zion, to give unto them beauty for ashes."   —Isa. 61:3

"New lamps for old," sang out the vendor in an Arabian street.

We know that this man was not unselfish. He was hoping to find the magic lamp of Aladdin. But he did start the "trade in" idea.

Papers urge us to trade in old radios, old TV's, old refrigerators, and old cars for new ones.

But listen to God's trade-in offer: "Beauty for ashes!"

The ashes of sorrow—the ashes of disappointment—the ashes of failure—the ashes of suffering —the ashes of increasing years: bring them all to God and go away with beauty. It seems too good to be true—but it is true.

For the ashes of sorrow—the beauty of the new growth out of the pruned spot in life. Was it not so with Job?

For the ashes of disappointment—the beauty of the forward look. Abram was disappointed in Ur, but he went forth to the city of God.

For the ashes of failure—the beauty of a new

41

start. Jonah failed when God called him first, but he was given a second chance and Nineveh was converted.

For the ashes of suffering—the beauty of fellowship with our suffering Saviour. "If we suffer, we shall also reign with him."

For the ashes of increasing years—the beauty of spiritual renewal, "I will renew their youth."

A fire illustrates our thought. Only when the ashes are cleared out do we get a bright, beautiful flame. Ashes are used to bank a fire so that it can only smolder. As the years go on the ashes of past things do accumulate.

How wise the one who heeds the call of God, "Beauty for ashes!"

For further certainty: Ps. 96.

A prayer: God of all loveliness, make me lovely, too. Help me to surrender to thee the ashes in my heart and soul. AMEN.

16. THE BEST OF WISDOM

"Who is a wise man and endued with knowledge among you? let him shew out of a good conversation his works with meekness of wisdom."

—Jas. 3:13

As children we knew how to make a huge snowball; it did not require much effort to simply stand at the top of a hill and roll a small handful of snow, and then start this bouncing down the hill. The farther it went, the larger the ball became. This was a natural process—everyone expected it. Snow clings to snow.

The world has this thought about wisdom. A child starts out with a small amount of wisdom. As he goes down the slope of life it is expected that more wisdom will cling to him. In age he will be greatly wise. Unhappily for us, this does not always follow. How often we find that our ball of foolishness is the one that grows in size through the years!

Wisdom comes by seeking. A poet has said, "it is wisdom to believe the heart." But what kind of heart? God has spoken to us of the meek, the lowly, the contrite heart. Such a heart bows before the surpassing wisdom of the heavenly Father. Such a heart recognizes how tiny is human understanding and knowledge. Such a heart turns in childlike faith and confidence to the Creator. If the years are to bring wisdom we shall find that this happens only by our growing conviction that of ourselves we know nothing.

We remember that Jesus spoke of himself as being "meek and lowly in heart," yet when he spoke all men marveled at his wisdom. As always, we study our Lord in order to find out the secrets of life which he would impart to us. If men found in him—as they did—more wisdom than they found in the professional wise men there was a reason. We shall find this reason by trying out the method of humility and patience. And after many years it may be that some wisdom will be ours!

For further enlightenment: Eccl. 7:11-22.

Let us pray: Our Father, we see thy glories around us, and we feel thy power in the world. Slowly we begin to know that we know not. Grant us the wisdom of the teachable heart. AMEN.

17. THE BEST OF TRUTH

"And ye shall know the truth, and the truth shall make you free." —John 8:32

Poor Pilate! With others he had studied deep subjects. He had wandered around the known world. He had talked to thousands of people. He had exercised power. But he could not find the truth. He had searched so long that he did not recognize truth when it came. As Jesus stood before him, this Roman governor asked his endless question, "What is truth?"

Now to those who were following him, Jesus had said plainly, "I am the truth." But to Pilate he could say only, "those who are of the truth hear my voice."

Do the passing days assure us that we are of the truth? Someone has suggested that truth must be dug out. While we dig through a mountain of mistakes and errors God is digging from the other side, and we are met halfway. The truth that we sought was that we shall see God himself. If we are faithful in our search we shall come nearer to this truth moment by moment.

An expression has become popular in our time: the "moment of truth." This is illustrated by the cruel sport of bullfighting. The bullfighter tantalizes the bull and side-steps the charging beast. But there comes the final moment: the sharp horns can be dodged no longer. Either the sword will slay the bull or the bull will slay the man.

And so it is with us too with this exception: when we are face to face with a critical illness or other rough crisis, we shall know the ultimate truth—our Saviour—and he will set us free.

What an immense sadness in the hollow echo of the centuries started by Pilate and kept alive by other doubters: "What is truth?" But what an immense gladness in the vibrant sounds from the very throne of God, "I am the truth." Today we continue our efforts to know him more and more fully.

Some precious truth in I John 1.

Turning the heart to God: O truth incarnate, O wisdom from on high, open my eyes to eternally real things. AMEN.

18. THE BEST OF HOUSES

"He that dwelleth in the secret place of the most High shall abide under the shadow of the Almighty."
—Ps. 91:1

In a story a man knew exactly the kind of house he would build one day. It would be a white house. It must be near the top of a hill. There must be adequate shade from lordly trees. A brook must flow nearby. The view must be superb. While he looked for this ideal spot, and while he saved money to build, the man grew older. Finally he came to the place of which he had dreamed, and he had sufficient funds laid aside. But before he could build, God called him home. Tragic? Not at all.

Although he had lived in inferior houses, he had the ideal house in his mind and heart. Actually he had been living in it and for it. It is the soul's house which counts and not the place where we eat and sleep.

That ideal place for our permanent home is in the secret place of the most high. It is well shaded by the shadow of the Almighty.

Are we of one mind with Abraham? His house in Ur was not his ideal. He went out to seek a city where he could be content, for he sought the city of God.

Augustine said, "We are restless, until we rest in Thee, O God." As grateful as we are for the hallowed homes on earth, made precious by love and laughter and pain, they are not enough.

One day when the disciples were discouraged, one asked Jesus: "We have forsaken all . . . what shall we have?" And Jesus said that any who forsake *houses* shall have an hundredfold, and, in addition, eternal life to dwell in the mansion prepared. We shall not be as the man who found his hilltop site too late.

How we search for the house not made with hands, eternal in the heavens! Even now we know this about it: it will be in the kingdom of God, it will be in the neighborhood of all choice souls, its value will never depreciate, our joy in it will never be less than radiant.

A promise of the best house in John 14:1-14.

Now to pray, My Lord, knowing that the place to lay the head is of minor importance, make me sure of the everlasting mansion. AMEN.

48

19. THE BEST OF PEACE

"Peace I leave with you, my peace I give unto you: not as the world giveth, give I unto you.

—John 14:27

Digging the Panama Canal brought forth many problems. But the greatest difficulty of all arose when landslides continued to occur at one spot. Time after time the dirt and rocks were dredged out of the canal bed. And time after time new landslides threw tons of earth and stone in the way of progress.

Finally, a famous engineer was called in consultation. He studied the situation. And then he said, "Your trouble is over. The hill has now reached the 'angle of repose.'"

That is true peace—the angle of repose. It takes us years to come to this situation, but that is what our Lord intended for us. The stubborn wills, the ambitious striving after nonessentials, the selfishness, the vanity, the needless fears—when these reach the angle of repose we know God's peace.

Is this not what is meant by one of our favorite verses: "In quietness and confidence shall be your strength, saith the Lord"? This kind of faith brings the angle of repose to the most turbulent soul.

And this too: when Chile and Argentina decided to end (once and for all) their needless wars, they planned a statue of Christ. A magnificent figure was erected on the Andes range between the two countries. We may forget however that the Christ of the Andes is made of melted cannon.

The best of peace, the peace of God, is not composed of milk-toast materials. The best of peace requires the same vigor, the same conviction, the same enthusiasm that we are willing to throw into warfare. Spears make wonderful pruning hooks, and swords make magnificent ploughs!

A further investigation in Luke 2:25-32.

Communion: I turn to thee, thou prince of peace. May my strivings be quieted. May the best of me be changed into the strength of thy peace. AMEN.

20. THE BEST OF LEGACIES

"He that overcometh shall inherit all things; and I will be his God, and he shall be my son."

—Rev. 21:7

Have you ever envied a monkey? In 1959 many of us had a feeling of envy for the two monkeys that were shot into outer space and returned to earth alive and well. What marvels they must have passed through!

But before they entered into that great inheritance of God's creation they had to be overcomers. They had to overcome the dangerous firing of the rocket. They had to overcome the changes in gravitational pull. They had to be triumphant over rapid acceleration and deceleration. They had to withstand extreme cold and extreme heat.

The best of legacies have conditions hedging them about. Many provide that the heir must reach legal maturity—he must overcome childhood and youth.

Others provide for a high standard of virtue—the heir must overcome his lower nature. And some insist that the heir or heiress remain unmarried until a certain age—desire must be controlled.

The best of God's legacies come with conditions.

Even Jesus had to overcome the world before he returned to his place at the right hand of the Father. Moses failed of his inheritance of the earthly promised land because of disobedience. Paul had to be faithful unto death to reach out for the "crown of righteousness" laid up for him. We are called "heirs of God and joint heirs with Christ" only if we take a share in the suffering and cross-bearing.

But how worthwhile it is!

The legacy is made up of all things that are of God. And who could describe what that will be like! To get a faint idea of our magnificent future we may name some of the things which are Christ's (inasmuch as we are fellow heirs with him): to be in God's presence continually; to be immune to sin and death; to be free of sorrow and suffering; to be given something to do eternally for the heavenly Father.

Substantiation of our hope in Acts 20:28-35.

A word with God: O Lord of the unsearchable riches, remember me. As I have been named an heir of thine, help me to overcome my temptations. Give me courage and patience. AMEN.

21. THE BEST OF FOOD

"It is written, Man shall not live by bread alone, but by every word that proceedeth out of the mouth of God." —Matthew 4:4

There was a day when the disciples left Jesus sitting on the rim of an old well in Samaria while they went away to get food for their journey. When they came back they urged him to eat. But he said, "I have meat to eat that ye know not of . . . my meat is to do the will of him that sent me." In the absence of the twelve our Lord had been about his father's business by preaching and witnessing to the woman of Samaria and her companions.

Certainly, Jesus did not disdain the physical food necessary to keep his earthly body rigorous, and he taught us to pray, "Give us this day our daily bread." His teaching was that food for the body is not the best of food inasmuch as the body is not the best of us. Our Lord was urging us to satisfy the deep hunger which three meals a day can never touch.

One of the beatitudes expresses the same thought: "Blessed are they that do hunger and thirst after righteousness, for they shall be filled." Righteousness is one of the items on our spiritual menu.

How shall we find the best of food then? The answer is that everyone of God's words is nourishment to the soul. The Bible continues to be a best seller because its pages help us to hear the words of God.

And we are helped even more than this since that starry night in Bethlehem so long ago. It was there that God's word became flesh and dwelt with men. Indeed, Jesus said of himself, "I am that bread of life."

How encouraging it is as the years go on that no poverty or other misfortune of life, no loss of appetite can take from us our portion of the bread of life. Our souls may be well-fed day after day as we ponder over the life of our Saviour and take his every word and deed into our longing souls.

Another mention of God's food in Acts 14:8-18.

Praying: Our Father, who art in heaven, give us this day our daily bread from heaven. AMEN.

22. THE BEST OF THOUGHT

"Bringing into captivity every thought to the obedience of Christ." —II Cor. 10:5

Wild horses range the western plains. But they are fewer than they were fifty or one hundred years ago. Man has brought the rollicking, aimless, and destructive animals into captivity. Now they have their share in the work of the world; now they are sure of care in the hard winter; now they belong.

How wild can our thoughts be! Like the horses wandering here and there and racing to no purpose mile after mile—thoughts can go untamed. The untamed thoughts of men and women have been the plague of mankind. Thoughts of world conquest in the minds of Caesar, Alexander, Napoleon, and others have wrought great havoc. And we remember that the thought of racial supremacy in the mind of Hitler plunged the nations into horrible conflict, and destroyed millions of Jewish people. In our own souls we must have seen the misery brought about by our untamed thinking.

Surely, the best of thought must be that brought into the wholesome captivity which is obedience to Christ. If the years bring us nothing else than this, that our every thought will be subject to the approval of our Lord, then we shall be blessed indeed.

How filled with stirring thoughts was the mind of Saul! And how he followed his galloping thoughts! No Christian was safe when Saul began to think. But after Saul had had his vision of the Lord on the way to Damascus—what a difference! His mind was no less full of surging thoughts, but they were brought into the obedience of Christ. As Paul, his thoughts turned the world right side up for God.

"A penny for your thoughts?" offers an idle friend.

"My life for your thoughts!" is the offer of the Saviour.

And, to go on, read Eccl. 12:8-14.

Today's prayer thought: Our Father, I know that as a man thinketh in his heart, so is he. Grant me the power to put my mind and heart under thee. AMEN.

23. THE BEST OF STRENGTH

"The joy of the Lord is your strength."—Neh. 8:10

An old truth known by Nehemiah and Ezra so long ago is being revived in our day: There is strength through joy. But when this truth is used to advocate the building of great muscles and physical stamina, it is but a partial truth. Our text expresses the whole truth: the best of strength comes through the joy of the Lord.

If we seek to test ourselves to see whether or not we have this strength we might use Isaiah's formula: "Their strength is to sit still." He was speaking to people in a time of great peril, and to a people that wondered whether or not they should go down to Egypt to get help. All with the joy of the Lord in their souls would be brave enough to "sit out" the crisis; those without this joy would flee in panic.

Let us see how this worked out in a small, Austrian village. The dreaded soldiers of Napoleon approached this town on a beautiful, sunny morning. The people knew that they were too weak to defeat this great body of rough men. After some thought, the elders of the village ordered the church bells to be rung. When the sound of the bells ringing gaily, gladly, came to the commanding general he called a halt to his advance. He said to his officers that a village as small as that would never ring the bells in such happy triumph unless they had a force strong enough to defeat him. And he marched his men off in another direction for fear of falling into a trap.

This is the kind of thing which can happen to us who find our greatest joy in our Lord. Illness may come, but we do not give up in panic; age may creep on, but we do not despair; losses are ours, but we do not surrender. We have the strength to sit still and wait for the salvation of the Lord. There are more with us than against us.

How wonderful to be so strong in the joy of our Lord that we dare, always, to sit still and not run from the assorted happenings of life! We may take a leaf from Paul's book. That great apostle made nothing of shipwreck, stonings, hunger, cold, imprisonment, but always he cried out, "Rejoice!"

About true strength: II Cor. 12:1-10.

Prayer time: O Lord, whose strength is made perfect in weakness, may thy joy course through me until I am truly strong. AMEN.

24. THE BEST OF GOODNESS

"But the fruit of the Spirit is . . . goodness."

—Gal. 5:22

A child plants a seed, and tomorrow he runs to see if there is a flower!

But the years have taught us how much time is wrapped up in the word *fruit*. The sun rises and sets often between seedtime and harvest. If this is true of apples and pears, of zinnias and hollyhocks —is it not true, also, of the fruits of the Spirit?

There is a small painting entitled, "Being Good." In it a young lad is shown in a chair with somber face and folded hands. He has been commanded to "be good" and there he sits. But out of the corner of his eye he is sizing up some choice opportunities for tricks and mischief! Goodness does not come so easily.

Many years ago, we humbly believe, the Spirit of the living God was planted in our souls. And now we must be in the vintage years when the fruits of the Spirit will be seen in us. Goodness is so important to the world, and our goodness is of special importance to others. Phillips Brooks said, "No man or woman of the humblest sort can really be strong, gentle, pure, and good, without the world being better for it, without somebody being helped and comforted by the very existence of that goodness." What a thrill it is to come to the age when we can be sure of our own goodness, and how we shall react to the crises of life!

The man in the parable had bought a yoke of oxen and he could not wait until he tried them out. How would they respond to tugs on the line or to his voice crying to them? How steadily would they pull? Could he safely leave them standing?

Again, how marvelous to come to the point where we know what we will do when trials come! The Spirit has borne its fruit.

For more, Rom. 15:1-14.

And to say, Lord, I long to be perfectly whole. May my goodness come to full flower in these days. AMEN.

25. THE BEST OF GLADNESS

"Thou has put gladness in my heart, more than in the time that their corn and their wine increased."

—Ps. 4:7

Gladness shows through. So we speak of a glad world when the sky is blue, the flowers are blooming, and everything fairly glitters. Humorously, we call gay clothing our "glad rags."

A drizzly, dreary day makes us picture the world as sad. And when we put on black or somber garments the world thinks of us as less than happy.

What is it that makes the difference? Doctors are inclined to think that the physical or mental condition controls sadness or gladness. They use new drugs to relieve depression, and the nurses, as they dispense the medicine, call them "happy pills." The thought is that we can be glad in any condition if we have that *something* which the drug supplies.

We have noticed this: walking from the bedside to the window does not bring gladness ordinarily. But how wonderful it seems to a person who has been flat on his back from illness or injury for many days! Few of us are glad because of common bread and butter, but the one who has been without food

61

for a day or two thinks he has never tasted anything so delicious. It must be then that things or conditions do not bring gladness. Our attitude toward them is the answer.

And a "happy pill" is a very poor substitute for deep-down gladness. We need an inner quality which will put a value on all things. It is this inner quality which God gives us. He gives true gladness. When God gives that gladness it is based on something better than an abundance of food and drink —the corn and wine.

Here again is a treasure which may come with maturity. Things rarely get better from a practical viewpoint. Things may even get worse. But deep within is the attitude toward God's smallest gifts which takes them as tokens of his eternal love.

With a glow read, Acts 2:40-47.

And pray: My heavenly Father, may there sing through my soul the words of the hymn, "Glad day! Glad day!" AMEN.

26. THE BEST OF PATIENCE

"Rest in the Lord, and wait patiently for him."
—Ps. 37:7

"Why don't we go?" asked the child in the train. And she rocked back and forth on the seat as though that would put the car in motion.

"It is not time," answered her mother. "The train leaves at three, and—see my watch—we have five minutes to wait."

"I don't care—*I'm* ready. Oh, why don't we go!"

"But look—there is a man hurrying to get on. If the train had started too early the poor fellow would have missed it."

"But *I'm* waiting—please tell the man to make us go."

How much of childhood and youth is spent in that anguished way! Why don't things "go" when we want them to go? Why does God keep us waiting? The world is so slow! And then, as the years go on, we are blessed with the rhythm of life. And how much happier we are! We think more often of the verse, "First the blade, then the ear, then the full corn in the ear." One thing must follow another.

In a story, a man of ninety-four was growing impatient. He said that he had done his life's work, he had seen his family and friends go—why couldn't he die and be at rest? And then, in that last year, a lawsuit was tried, and this man was the only one who knew some facts; his testimony in court righted a great wrong. With awe he recognized that he had been spared to do this good thing.

We are told to wait patiently for the Lord, just as the prophet Habakkuk went up on his watch tower and waited and nothing happened. He wanted a vision, and God said, "Though it tarry, wait for it. It will surely come."

Our long experience with God brings patience, for we have found that he can be depended upon. In his perfect time, he comes, and in his accepted time, he does for us every good thing.

And so we read, Heb. 10:31-39.

Adding the prayer, O Lord of the still small voice, may I demand less and less the wind, the earthquake, and the fire. AMEN.

27. THE BEST OF REJOICING

"Notwithstanding in this rejoice not, that the spirits are subject unto you; but rather rejoice, because your names are written in heaven." —Luke 10:20

Ozymandias is not a name we would give to a baby! Indeed, who would give it to a puppy or a kitten? But, many centuries ago, a king bore this name and was proud of it.

So proud of his name was Ozymandias that he carved it on a great stone pillar, which he erected in the land. He rejoiced because he had defeated many nations, he rejoiced that he ruled many people, and he rejoiced that he had made his name so famous.

But many years passed. The city crumbled. The pillar toppled. The sand covered the inscription. Generations later archeologists uncovered the monument and read the dim lettering. They asked, "Who in the world was this Ozymandias? We have never heard of him."

In earlier years, we rejoice that things are subject to us, we rejoice in our successes, and we rejoice that affairs depend upon us. We flex our muscles!

And then, we slowly discern that none of this is

permanent. Instead of rejoicing that our names are seen of men, we begin to understand we could share the fate of Ozymandias. We take thought to make our hearts right with God. So that we arrive at the best of rejoicing. We rejoice that our names are written in heaven.

If God knows our names, how secure we are! Then we need not fear that our life's fame will be nothing but a broken pillar in a sand-swept desert. We shall not dread that the account of what we have done will be a mystery to those who come after us.

We rejoice that because our names are written in heaven, the Father will know us as we struggle toward him and will say, "This is my son who was lost and is found."

A helpful portion, Isa. 61:7-11.

Prayerful thinking: O eternal and everlasting One, know me. Know my name, forever, O Lord. AMEN.

28. THE BEST OF FAITH

"Now faith is the substance of things hoped for, the evidence of things not seen." —Heb. 11:1

A new grandchild has arrived. But the baby chose to be born in California and grandmother and grandfather live in Maine. The grandparents may boast to the neighbors that there is a little boy on the west coast—the latest addition to their family. But where is the evidence? Some weeks later a picture comes. Ah, there is proof! No doubt now about the infant. See how chubby he is, and how much hair he has!

Faith is like that picture. The Bible lists many promises of blessed things to come, and preachers preach about them. Books of speculation are written. But where is the evidence? And then, in our innermost souls, a true image of God and his goodness and his purpose in the world takes shape. This faith slowly but surely drives away doubt.

But like a picture faith does not come suddenly. First, the soul must be exposed to God's truth, then there is a time of developing and, finally, the enlargement through the years. Young faith is admirable, but young faith cannot be so clear as mature faith.

Of course we put the picture away sometimes and begin to worry about our situation and our future, but we cannot be seriously anxious, for we know where the picture is. We know that we have a tried faith.

Walt Whitman is credited with the saying, "faith is the antiseptic of the soul." When we cut a finger and open our blood stream to the infection of the outside world we hurry to pour an antiseptic on the wound. When our souls are cut by doubt and we are in danger of being invaded by the world's despair, faith is our sure medicine.

More about faith, Gal. 3:1-12.

Faith in prayer: Loving heavenly Father, I believe. Help thou mine unbelief. AMEN.

29. THE BEST OF FORGIVENESS

"For if you forgive men their trespasses, your heavenly Father will also forgive you." —Matt. 6:14

How happy a prisoner who could name his own sentence, or a condemned man who could decide whether he should be put behind bars for life or be set free! And yet, every child of God has that privilege.

Through the years we have realized how true is the statement, "All have sinned and come short of the glory of God." We have no alibi, we have no excuse, and we know how many times we have been wrong. What then?

Decide for yourselves! Our heavenly Father invites us to do so. If we will forgive the wrongs done to us by other people, then God will match our forgiveness in overlooking the wrongs we have done to him.

That is not easy, but it is easier to all who have been spared to mature years. The years bring a truer perspective. A visitor to an art gallery who stands close to an oil painting may think the work crude and imperfect. But let him step back to the proper distance and he will see how few and unimportant are the errors. The wrongs we thought we had suffered do not seem so great as time goes on —and we forgive sincerely.

And God intends us to forgive ourselves, among others. Jowett explained this:

There is the sin of a far-off yesterday, of which we have repented, and which we have confessed, and which the gracious Lord has forgiven, and yet we turn to it again and again with heavy and unrelieved heart. We go back and dig it up again when the Lord Himself has buried it, and when over its grave He has planted fair heartsease and lilies of peace.

Additional light, Col. 3:12-17.

In prayer: O Lord God, I do not think of thee as an angry judge, but as a loving Father. If I have unforgiveness against any, help me to rid myself of it. AMEN.

30. THE BEST OF COMFORT

"As one whom his mother comforteth, so will I comfort you; and ye shall be comforted."—Isa. 66:13

Before Jesus went to the cross, he prepared his disciples. He told them that the Comforter would come *after* he had gone. They were not to be alone for one minute. It was necessary for him to leave them, but the Holy Spirit would come to do for them what he had been doing.

This comforting action of Jesus is something like the mother of a household going around the home lighting the lamps *before* darkness falls. When darkness comes the children will not be frightened because they were told of it in advance, and the lamps are glowing to combat the shadows.

Is not this the way God comforts us—his people? Without waiting until we are plunged in deep despair, he tells us of the perils of life, its troubles, its heartbreaks, and its losses. And he promises to be with us "alway, even unto the end of the world."

And as a mother gives the best of comfort by gathering the bruised child in her arms, so does God promise that, "underneath are the everlasting arms." It is comforting for a child to have his dirty face scrubbed, to have his hungry stomach filled, to have clean clothes, and to have his tears wiped away. But the best comfort is the love which his mother bestows upon him.

We may boast of our independence, of our maturity, of how well we can take care of ourselves. But, no matter how old we get, our hearts are child-like when pain and trouble come. It is said that when Rudyard Kipling was critically ill in the hospital in a foreign city he was heard to mutter something. The nurse asked what he wanted. The reply, "I want my heavenly Father." How blessed to know that God is ever near with comfort even greater than that of a kind mother!

And we read on, Isa. 49:13-16.

With prayer: Our Father, the scriptures have been called "comfortable words." May they ever be so to me. AMEN.

31. THE BEST OF REVERENCE

"The place whereon thou standest is holy ground."
—Exod. 3:5

The woman of Samaria had a trick question: she asked Jesus if God was to be worshiped there in their mountain—or must he be worshiped in Jerusalem? The Lord replied that neither place was necessary, since God must be worshiped in spirit and in truth.

Reverence is so often confined to our temples; it is in a church we bow down . . . we call it a holy place. But God said to Moses, "The place whereon thou standest is holy ground."

No matter where we happen to be at this moment, no matter where life has brought us—we are on God's holy ground.

When Martin Luther was on trial for his faith, he said, "Here I stand . . . I can do no other . . . God helping me." The pavement of that courtroom was holy ground for Luther.

If we believe (as we do) that we are called to follow the Saviour, if we believe (as we do) that God is using us to do great works for the kingdom through mankind, every step is on holy ground.

Wherever God is is bound to be holy ground.

And where can we go from God? The psalmist faced that question:

> Whither shall I go from thy spirit?
> or whither shall I flee from thy presence?

And he answers himself that he cannot go where God is not. Darkness and light are filled with God. On the sea or on the land, God is near. Heaven or hell make no difference.

If the years restrict our field of operations even to one room—that is holy ground. Indeed, the years seem to act as a whirlpool. Each year circling brings us nearer to the center of reverence. Each year draws us closer to the immediate presence of God. No matter how drab or how painful the place I now occupy—it is holy ground.

In the same spirit, Ps. 33:1-9.

With a prayer, Holy, holy, holy, art thou, O Lord. Help me to cast off the shoes of my discontent that I may not defile this holy ground. AMEN.

32. THE BEST OF CONTENTMENT

"Not that I speak in respect of want: for I have learned, in whatsoever state I am, therewith to be content." —Phil. 4:11

Divine Discontent—? Well, perhaps there is such a thing, but there is a divine contentment, too.

When Paul was shipwrecked on an island, he had discontent at the thought of his delayed work for God, but he had complete contentment of heart. He knew that this mishap was in God's keeping; he knew that some great good would come of it.

The best of contentment is to come to the point of being content in any circumstance.

A bridge, put across a great river, that is made for good weather only is not safe. The year is bound to bring high winds. The seasons will bring frost, snow, rain. The sun will not shine always. The dews of night will cause rust. A good bridge is made to withstand all weather changes.

Contentment cannot be godly if it depends on ideal circumstances. A contentment not designed to withstand coming age, illness, loss of work, sorrow, and bereavement is worthless.

Think of a mystery story, and how the hero or

heroine gets into the worst possible situations. How in the world is it all coming out? To help us as we read, clues are planted here and there. Here is a hint as to the reason why the hero is in such trouble, and here is another (if we can see it) to explain the author's plan.

Contentment comes when we are sure of the outcome of life. Indeed, there is a real satisfaction in looking for the clues. For we can be sure that all things are working out for good for us.

Each step on the desert that separates us from the promised land brings us nearer our destination. Why not be joyfully content as we journey on?

Beyond the text, Phil. 4:12-19.

Ask and receive: Father God, thou wilt send me things to do and things to think this day and night. May I be well pleased to serve thee. AMEN.

33. THE BEST OF GIVING

"Freely ye have received, freely give."

—Matt. 10:8

The old well was more than a hundred years old, and it had served the farm families without failing. It never was so full that it overflowed the well top, nor did it ever dry up to the point of giving less than enough. Other wells in the vicinity were guilty of both extremes. Some had overflowed the top of the shaft and flooded out the gardens, while others went so dry that no pumping by hand or machine could bring up a drop of water. The faithful old well gave freely.

Is it not possible that freely means without friction? Sometimes, especially when a great and good cause needs money, we think "freely" means a great sum. And we are sorrowful because we cannot give much. But if freely giving is giving without boast or complaint, giving naturally, then we can do that.

And is not that the way we have received? When God gave manna to the people wandering in the wilderness, he gave enough for the day and no more. And they were told to avoid trying to preserve a supply for the day following. God gives us, and we receive, our regular need of courage, faith, hope, and physical strength for the day. There is no over-plus, no lack. Freely he gives to us—freely we receive.

The best of giving, of course, is the giving of ourselves. This kind of giving is learned through the years. Earlier in life we think that money is what we must give, or things that money will buy. Gradually we learn that people and causes, the world and God, need us more than they need our possessions. If we have admitted that God has supplied all our needs—our understanding of giving freely—then we feel our joyful obligation to supply today's needs by expending ourselves.

Yes, freely our Lord gave himself, and freely we received him. If freely we give ourselves day by day, then freely shall we be received in heaven day by day until we are lost in God.

How to give ourselves: Matt. 25:34-40.

Giving in prayer: O Lord, take me as I give myself. May I not give by fits and starts, but may I give freely. AMEN.

34. THE BEST OF SACRIFICE

"Present your bodies a living sacrifice, holy, acceptable unto God, which is your reasonable service."
—Rom. 12:1

In the story, *Around the World in Eighty Days,* a seacaptain finds that his fuel is exhausted. There is no coal or wood to throw on the dying fire, and consequently the ship is slowing down many miles away from port. What can be done?

The captain did this: he burned the ship, piece by piece. The cabins went into the fire, the railing following, and then the masts and the bowsprit. Everything but the bare hull, the rudder, the paddle wheels and the helm was sacrificed. But the ship made her way to port, and her gallant mission was accomplished.

Surely this is a lesson for us all. Through the years we think we are sacrificing. We give time to the work of God. We give our money as we can spare it. Our abilities are shared with the kingdom. A son or daughter may be given to missionary labors in dangerous fields. But at the last will we give our bodies in order to complete our voyage for our Lord?

The devil in the Book of Job makes this same point. He thinks it is possible that Job will endure through the loss of property. He even thinks Job will remain steadfast when his children are taken. But, he suggests, if Job's own body is touched? As we read the story we can see that the devil was almost right in his opinion. Job came close to losing his faith.

How to give the body? By denying its wants and desires. The body craves painlessness; it craves sufficient food and a bit over; it craves ease. The body has appetites; it has fears.

To prepare the body for a sacrifice unto the eternal is to cleanse it of all needless urges. In brief, the body must become subject to God and the soul. The body must not be the master. As Emily Dickinson puts it:

> To put this world down like a bundle
> And steady walk away

Some holy thoughts, Ps. 51.

Joined to prayer: Help me, my God, to refuse to be content in sacrificing that which costs me nothing. AMEN.

35. THE BEST OF POSSIBILITY

"Jesus said unto him, If thou canst believe, all things are possible to him that believeth."—Mark 9:23

How fast a healthy baby crawls! And how he tries to pull himself up! This energy and confidence will inspire someone to say, "It is possible that he will be walking soon."

But when an adult has lost the power to walk from the effects of accident or illness, and the doctor says, "It is entirely possible that you will walk again," the patient rarely has the same will to move that the baby has. This will is necessary. Our Lord said that possibility is limited only by belief. One of the blessings of the years is the opening up of greater possibilities based on faith.

In the old story of, "The Great Stone Face," the boy Ernest is fascinated to think that a man will come one day who will look exactly like the face on the cliff. His soft boyish features are nothing like that majestic face, but each year of work and sacrifice makes the maturing Ernest a little more like the face. In age the likeness is exact.

Certain things must be endured, certain things must be done, a certain road must be traveled. Then possibility is at its best. We have sent so many ships out to sea that they must start coming back to us. We have written so many letters to life that answers are bound to arrive regularly.

One of the most delightful of Dickens' characters is Micawber. That roly-poly man will never admit defeat; all disasters are temporary, and hardships are trifles. Why? Because "something is bound to turn up." Something does turn up, and Micawber's faith is repaid. He gets his chance of a new life in a new land.

How much more will this be done to those of us who believe in God! All good things can happen, all good things will happen!

A lesson, Mark 10:17-27.

I pray: Father God, to whom nothing is impossible, open the doors even beyond my feeble faith. AMEN.

36. THE BEST OF LIFE

"And this is the record, that God hath given to us eternal life, and this life is in his Son."

—I John 5:11

"Your Children Will Live to Be 150 Years Old!" What a lovely title this was for a magazine article! It was based on sober statistics, as the author pointed out that within two or three generations our life expectancy has increased by thirty years. Hence, at the same rate of improvement, our children may well expect 150 years of good life.

But this is childish in view of our *real* life expectancy. Since the coming of our Lord, our guaranteed life term is nothing short of eternal. This means, of course, that our life will never end.

And yet, our life must enter a new and everlasting environment. We have proof of this as our powers decline physically and become more spiritual year after year. Automatically, life is preparing for the eternal habitation.

Perhaps this may be clearer to us if we think of the parachute jumpers in an airplane. They sit on the benches until jump time, and then, in turn, they move toward the door. Before they jump they hook their parachute cord to the "static line" in order that the parachute may open in due time and save them from death.

In this world we dwell cosily with our fellow men. But each of us moves toward the door. We have found that eternal life is in our Lord, and before we go out to the unknown we hook our hopes to him. Safely, then, we may launch forth knowing that our salvation is not in doubt.

How good we have found life in this world! But how much better we may expect it to be in the larger world! Paul knew this in his day. He loved life here—"It is Christ to live," he said, then remembering his vision on the road to Damascus, he said, "But to die is great gain."

More about life, John 3:1-15.

A life prayer: Lord of the living and not of the dead, God of Abraham, Isaac, and Jacob, make me see that my life is one—there is no death. AMEN.

37. THE BEST OF INTENTIONS

"For which of you, intending to build a tower, sittest not down first, and counteth the cost, whether he have sufficient to finish it?" —Luke 14:28

The unfinished leaves us in agony. An unfinished symphony, for instance—what grand climax might have stirred us to the depths? Or a book found unfinished on an author's desk—would right have triumphed in the end? We feel that we have been defrauded. In a way we are like the hapless travelers who come to a certain river in the eastern section of the United States with the intent to cross to the other side. There is a bridge, but there are no approaches on either side to make possible driving or walking across.

Unfinished works were started with the best of intentions, but whoever started them did not reckon on the cost. How much effort must be committed, how much time expended, how much money spent? Beyond all this, and most important, how much life must be available?

How guilty we all are in this regard! A great deed was started, a great life work was begun, a magnificent dream was put into the loom of fancy. And now we look backward across the years and are startled to behold so much unfinished. Many bridges for God and mankind stand uncompleted.

But there is great hope for us. The years also have brought us to what are, really, the best of intentions. We have learned, finally, our limitations, and we have learned at the same time that God is unlimited. Now we plan on a scale possible to us as we find ourselves, and we are able to finish what we begin.

In this part of our life there is nothing more fascinating than to watch how God works with us and through us. He can take the small deed, the human career and magnify them beyond imagining. The young lad who brought his lunch of loaves and fishes when Jesus was preaching had no intention of feeding thousands of people, but the Lord took what he had and multiplied it.

About intentions, Heb. 4.

Addressing God: My Father, may my desire to do great things for thee be extravagant, but may my performance be in the spirit of humility that I may finish the work given me to do. AMEN.

38. THE BEST OF EQUALITY

"But by an equality, that now at this time your abundance may be a supply for their want, that their abundance also may be a supply for your want: that there may be equality." —II Cor. 8:14

A frequent cry of peddlers in former years was, "What do you lack?" The implication was that no householder could possibly have an ample supply of everything needed for a family's use. The point of course was well-taken. As a housewife took stock of her possessions she was bound to find an empty shelf, bin, or cupboard.

Even so the peddler was trying to give a one-sided picture. His business was selling and not buying, and he would not dream of adding to his cries, "And of what do you have a surplus?"

In order to strike an equality in our lives we need to look at both sides of this picture. There is no one so poor in one regard that he is not rich in another, nor is there one so rich that he is not poor in some direction. One of God's great blessings is that his gifts are not identical to all. If this were so we would have no need of one another, for everyone would be sufficient unto himself. It is a happy thing, and a godly thing to complete ourselves with others and to complete others with ourselves.

As an illustration let us think of the retired professor whose income was small and inadequate. He had a neighbor—a farmer—whose fields and gardens supplied more than the farm family needed. This farmer shared his surplus with the professor. On his part, the professor found that farmer's education was not great enough to enable him to keep an accurate set of books; therefore the professor was privileged to use his mathematical skill to help the farmer.

The apostle Paul had a vision of all Christians giving themselves to the extent that none would lack life's essentials, or wisdom, or knowledge, or vision, or opportunity.

Surely, the best of equality is to be wise enough to know what we need from God's other children and to know what surplus we have to share.

Read with understanding: Matt. 20:1-15.

This, or your own prayer: I am remembering, my God, the One who, while he was rich, made himself poor for my sake that both of us might be one with thee. AMEN.

39. THE BEST OF GROWTH

"Thus hath the Lord God shewed unto me; and, behold, he formed grasshoppers in the beginning of the shooting up of the latter growth; and, lo, it was the latter growth after the king's mowings."

—Amos 7:1

How important is the latter growth! The prophet Amos, in order to show how completely desolate was the land, says the latter growth was destroyed. Loss of the early growth was bad—but to lose the latter growth, that would be fatal. And with people as with crops.

In college a young man was careless. His lessons were poorly done, for he cared more for fun than work. His appearance was untidy. Privately, his friends voted him "Least Likely to Succeed." But after he went out into life something happened to him. He changed—worked hard, and became dependable. Eventually, this poor scholar became the president of a missionary training school. He has left behind him a name and fame. He had the latter growth.

Paul hammered at this thought of the latter growth. How often he closed his letters with, "Grow in grace . . . grow in the knowledge of Jesus Christ . . . grow . . . grow . . . grow."

The latter years of a person's life are always the most important to God. Then is the growth more truly spiritual and of eternal value.

Nor do we ever pass beyond the period of this best of growth. As the ancient warrior and traveler, Ulysses, urged his men to get into the boat and pull strongly at the oars, he said, "It is not too late to seek a newer world." He said it was his purpose to sail beyond the sunset.

The coming sunset does not frighten us. The latter growth with God goes beyond that sunset.

And so we read II Pet. 3:9-18.

In prayer: Dear Lord, kind Lord, my soul is shaken with the thought that I can improve. Help me with the latter growth. AMEN.

40. THE BEST OF BOASTING

"For if I have boasted any thing to him of you, I am not ashamed; but as we spake all things to you in truth, even so our boasting, which I made before Titus, is found a truth." —II Cor. 7:14

Bragging and boasting are not the same. Bragging is self-centered—we are familiar with bragging— "my car is better than your car. My father is smarter than your father. My family came over in the May-flower."

But boasting can be about other people. Paul boasted about the Corinthians to Titus; Paul was so happy with the good qualities of his converts that he could not resist telling someone.

In the stonecutting trade the workmen use the term "boast." This means the rough shaping of a stone with a chisel to *prepare for finer work.* It is amazing how much encouragement a man, woman, or child can take from the boastful praises of someone who knows what he is talking about. We can prepare others for their finer work by giving them a commendation to others now and then.

And, as the years go on, are we not more and more impressed with the goodness and ability of our fellow man? How can we help but boast of them to anyone who will listen?

It seems that Paul was like doting grandparents. The grandmother or grandfather always has a picture of the grandchildren and no urging is needed to display the wonders of the boys and girls. Paul had every new Christian in his heart. He rejoiced to sing their virtues and promises.

Our Lord does the same for us before the Father. He calls us his own, and he loves us with an everlasting love.

In our day and time, there is a fine contribution to make by selecting the worthy folk in the world and boasting of them as the children of God.

Remembering, also, the words of the hymn:

> Forbid it Lord that I should boast
> Save in the death of Christ my God.

Helps for boasting, Ps. 44:1-8.

Supplication: Heavenly Father, may I rejoice in the true, the just, the lovely. May my boasting bear fruit. AMEN.

41. THE BEST OF COMPASSION

"Finally, be ye all of one mind, having compassion one of another, love as brethren, be pitiful, be courteous." —I Pet. 3:8

In the days when men were sent to the galleys as punishment, and when they were sentenced to long years chained to the oars, a clergyman named Spragg found himself chained to an oar with several members of his congregation. They had been accused of revolutionary acts against the king. A day came when it was discovered that Spragg was a minister and his captors offered him his release. However this man of God refused his freedom. He said that he could not walk about without his chain and in the sunlight when he knew that men of his flock were still bound. He was expressing compassion, which means to "suffer with."

In earlier life we do our best to sympathize with others in their need. We call upon the sick and bereaved, and we listen patiently to stories of heartbreak; truly, we do what we can. However if we do not know what it means to be chained to the oars to which they are chained, our compassion is incomplete.

The best of compassion comes after the years have brought us face to face with personal troubles. If we have had a hospital experience we can feel for others when they are confined. After we have lost a dear one we are prepared to console the bereaved. After we have been on the ragged edge financially we can know the desperation of the one who is out of funds.

In the valley of the shadow of death, it is Jesus who helps most, because he has suffered death in his turn, he has been to the far land and knows that it can be conquered.

Indeed every trouble is in a sense a strange country. The compassionate one is he who has traveled in that unknown land, for he can tell what may be expected there. When we can say to another who is entering into the shadows, "I have been through there. I know how you feel, and I can assure you that God will be with you all the way," we have the best of compassion. How happy we are when we can put our past suffering to the use of present sufferers!

Read Rom. 2: 1-11.

A prayer: Dear Lord, about Jesus I remember most his compassion. May I be compassionate now when I know what suffering is. AMEN.

42. THE BEST OF JUDGMENT

"Judge not, that ye be not judged." —Matt. 7:1

A wise old professor said to his pupils: "It is man's temptation to carry a little judgment seat around with him, and when he meets a new person he takes out that judgment seat. He places himself on it, he sizes up the stranger, and he gives his judgment. His words can never be erased from the world."

True, is it not? Without robe or courtroom each of us takes the right of the judge. But the Lord said that the best of judgment is no judgment!

Not many years ago, the son of a famous judge was arrested for theft. To the horror and surprise of the father his own boy was brought before his bench. After a shocked moment, the judge handed his gavel to a fellow judge. Then he stood before the bar of justice with his boy. He felt that the lad had inherited something from him which led him into error.

Perhaps this is the thought of Jesus. No one of us is perfect. If we judge another, we are giving judgment on ourselves.

As it was with David when the prophet came before him to complain of a rich man who had robbed a poor man of his one lamb. David judged the man guilty of death, and the prophet replied to David, "Thou art the man."

It takes some years before we are ready to admit that we are unable to see into the heart of a man. He may *seem* to us a lazy person. She may *seem* disloyal. But are we sure? The years teach us to examine our own hearts fearfully, and then we are ready to give the benefit of the doubt to all. God is the great judge. In his keeping we can place the fate of others. In his keeping our fate is as favorable as our mercy toward others.

An instance of the best of judgment, Rom. 2:1-11.

And say: O God, if my hasty judgment of others has hurt, forgive me and restore them. AMEN.

43. THE BEST OF THE KINGDOM

"Wherefore we receiving a kingdom which cannot be moved, let us have grace, whereby we may serve God acceptably with reverence and godly fear."

—Heb. 12:28

The world is wide, and heaven is immense. Awed by what we know to be God's creation, we comfort ourselves with the thought that all we can see and all beyond our sight is within the bounds of the kingdom our Lord came to declare. Is this, however, the kingdom which we have received?

Our answer is that we are possessed of a kingdom even greater than the one which humbles us by its wonder and size. The best of the kingdom is eternal, and that is what we have received.

Jesus spoke of the kingdom being within man. To think of being hosts to the kingdom of God must cause misgivings as well as pride. We may be helped in our understanding by remembering that sons and daughters are said to have their father in them. Even though Junior walks with his own legs and throws a ball with his own hands, observers can detect that the lad is moved by the same impulses which are seen in his father. The heritage is passed down from generation to generation, until there is a dynasty; among kings we speak of the Tudors, the Windsors, the Stuarts. Among Christians we say that the kingdom is within us.

And there is no doubt that each of us finds the best part of the kingdom of God within himself since that is all that he can rule over. In the parable of the ruler who found it necessary to make a trip to a far land we find that the sovereign left the responsibility with several servants and commanded, "Occupy until I come again."

That is where we find ourselves now—caring for a precious part of the kingdom which can never be moved. This gives us permanency and a future. In his graciousness, God has made us essential to the final triumph of light over darkness.

Day by day, and year after year, we salute our fellow kings and compare notes of our victories. And, altogether, we turn to the king of kings and acknowledge our stewardship.

For guidance, Col. 1:1-13.

And this prayer for an under ruler: O Lord of my life make me faithful as I set thy kingdom in order within me. AMEN.

44. THE BEST OF ZEAL

"Who gave himself for us, that he might redeem us from all iniquity, and purify unto himself a peculiar people, zealous of good works." —Tit. 2:14

Dickens wrote of a minister who counseled his congregation to "keep their hearts warm, their heads cool, and be enthusiastic over nothing!" What kind of life would it be without enthusiasm? Who is able to live day after day without getting excited about something? One of our greatest pleasures is to experience a burning zeal for some person or cause or hobby.

But the best of zeal, what would that be? What else but enthusiasm for the good works which our Lord has demonstrated to us and commanded us to do?

Frequently newspaper publishers take a poll of their readers to find out which of the pages are most widely read. The results show that the sports section stands high in popularity. The reason for this is the enthusiasm with which men and women follow the records of teams and athletes who are struggling to win and to show individual excellence. If this is true of worldly endeavor to excel marks made in the past, how much more should it be true of spiritual endeavor? Secretly, perhaps, but with zeal, each of us is trying to be outstanding in some Christian virtue and work, and each of us thrills to the accounts of some hero of the cross who has done nobly.

There was a time when we were new to the ranks of those who seek to build a new world—we were the clumsy recruits. Years have passed since then, and we are now professionals. Zeal becomes more and more intense as we find ourselves coming nearer to the high standards set for us in the New Testament. Like Caleb of old who, at the age of eighty-five, pleaded for a mountain to conquer, we rejoice that our strength to go out and do battle for good is stronger than it was in the beginning. We begin to understand the writer of old who cried, "The zeal for thy house hath eaten me up." Selfishness, and self-interest fade in the enthusiasm we feel for all that is God's.

Some words for warriors: I Cor. 14:1-12.

Prayer before battle: O Lord of hosts, the hosts of evil press around and within. Give me a stout heart and a burning zeal. AMEN.

45. THE BEST OF WITNESSING

"Having therefore obtained help of God, I continue until this day, witnessing both to small and great."
—Acts 26:22

There is no secret voting with God. In the United States I go to the polls to cast a ballot. I close curtains behind me, and I vote for the men of my choice. No one knows for whom I have voted. This is good for democracy, but, in the kingdom of God it is not so. Each of us must show himself on decision day. Whose side are we on?

Joshua put out the question to the Israelites: "Choose ye this day whom ye will serve."

Jesus put out the same question to his followers: "But whom do ye say that I am?"

We go through life answering that question to small and great: humble people and great people ask of us the answer, children and the aged put the question. Where we go answers—what we do answers—our words answer—our attitude of courage or despair will answer. Always, and ever, we are witnessing for our Lord and the right.

The best of witnessing is that done after many years. When a new paint is put on the market, a model house may be selected as a trial. Sensible buyers will not choose the paint just because it looks good on the first day, or even after the first year. The question is how will it stand up? Only years will say. The best witnessing of that house will be done after it has stood the weather for a number of seasons. So with God's witness.

Our best witnessing is now after we have admitted to the world that we have accepted our guidance from God, and that his program is our program. For younger people excuses are made because the yoke of Christ is quite new to them, but for us there is no excuse. People will wonder about us. Is their religion a surface thing? Is it peeling off as the storms of life beat upon it? Do they still believe? Are they eternally committed?

About witnessing: Luke 24:44-48.

Simply: Lord, I have seen and heard things in my soul. May my life publish abroad these things. AMEN.

46. THE BEST OF NAMES

"Him that overcometh will I make a pillar in the temple of my God, and he shall go no more out: and I will write upon him the name of my God."

—Rev. 3:12

A traveler sent his bags on ahead of him, and when he got to his hotel in France the clerk called him by name. But the name was not his real name, for the clerk addressed him as, "Mr. Genuine Cowhide." He had found this name on the luggage.

In a true sense we all send our bags ahead of us into the blessed land. The name found on that luggage will be the name by which we shall be known eternally.

Day by day we are committing some part of us into God's keeping. Paul recognized this. He said he was sure that God would take good care of all he had committed unto him. But not only will God take care of what we send ahead—he will know us by the luggage.

In the Gospels there is the story of the last judgment. Each nation, each person, had sent something on ahead. And no one knew that he had sent anything! Those who had sent kindness and mercy and pity were surprised to see these things there. And those who had sent selfishness, indifference, and cruelty were equally surprised. But each was known by what he had sent. And on what they had sent the names were found: "Blessed," "Accursed."

What will be the name placed on us? Will it be the best of names—the name of our God? We can be sure of this when everything we have done has borne that precious name. If, despite the weakness of our humanity, we have ascribed our daily work, our humble pleasures, our ambitions and our dreams to the name of our Redeemer we need have no misgivings.

Our luggage has not been perfect but we have called upon God to help us and bless us. We have lived in the shadow of that Name which is above every name. And we have the unbroken promise that we shall be like him. His name and sign we shall bear.

God honors his name, Isa. 43:17.

Longingly: O thou whose name has brought me out of darkness into marvelous light, make me thy child forever. AMEN.

47. THE BEST OF MEMORY

"I will remember the works of the Lord: surely I will remember thy wonders of old."   —Ps. 77:11

In one of Oliver Wendell Holmes' essays is this startling statement:

> Memory is a crazy witch;
> She treasures bits of rags and straw,
> And throws her jewels out of the window.

The best of memory will choose among things remaining. The rags and straw will go out of the window. The jewels will remain. And these jewels, as we grow older, are many and bright.

The best jewels are the works of the Lord which we have seen. As we sing sometimes:

> Count your many blessings
> See what God has done.

For, when we come right down to it, every blessing is something God has done.

The psalmist had in mind the many times he had been delivered from the enemy, the many times food and water had been provided in his need. The love of wife and children and his physical strength were in his memory.

Each has his own treasures to sort over. An aged woman was accustomed to put her valuables in a wooden chest. In moments of "blueness" she took out the things one by one. These were the simple gifts sent to her through the years: a card reminded her of a thoughtful friend, a bit of embroidery spoke of hours given to her by a sister. Little knick-knacks were there from children and grandchildren. From all of these mementos love rubbed off and made the dark days bright. She could have picked over the rags and straw of the days of illness and trouble and worry. But she was wise enough to fondle the jewels only.

Our memories become richer each year. The list of God's wonders becomes longer.

The other verses, Ps. 77.

Remembered prayer: Kind, heavenly father, my soul is full of thy goodness. Especially do I recall the sweet hours of prayer. AMEN.

48. THE BEST OF LIBERTY

"O Lord, truly am I thy servant . . . thou hast loosed my bonds." —Ps. 116:16

The psalmist makes a strange statement: "I am thy servant . . . thou hast loosed my bonds."

The best of liberty is freedom to choose a master. For do we not serve someone or something always?

A man or maid decides on matrimony. After that he or she is a servant to the one beloved. And he or she will feel that the other has loosed the bonds of loneliness and aimless desire. A girl chooses to be a teacher. Thereafter she is the servant of many children. But they loose her bonds of idleness and purposelessness. Parents become servants to their minor children. But their children loose their bonds of sadness and an interrupted heritage.

We look within and know our master. We know from what bonds that master has loosed us. We have chosen deliberately. But the little lords of family, work, hobbies seem so small when compared to our great allegiance. For the very best of liberty is to choose the Lord our God to serve him only.

And see how many bonds he looses: sin—death —sorrow—desperation—inner want—restlessness.

Across the years we look back to the time when we put our lives in the keeping of the eternal One. He spoke to us in terms such as we read on the Statue of Liberty base: "I lift my lamp beside the golden door." We have given ourselves to that Light of the World—Jesus. The door has been golden in freedom.

The years may bring bonds to the body and mind which we did not know in youth. But, at the same time, the years bring a greater sense of the great liberty which we have enjoyed. Even our present bonds will yield in time to the Lord of all life.

About true freedom, I Pet. 2:15-25.

Prayer of a free person: My Master, I know that I was a servant to sin and death. I know that I am free. Make me thine forever. AMEN.

49. THE BEST OF GREATNESS

"Thy gentleness hath made me great."

—II Sam. 22:36

A young shepherd boy was tending the sheep in the Apennines Mountains. To while away the time he was drawing a rude picture with some materials at hand. On a holiday, the great artist Cimabue was in the same territory. By pure chance he saw the boy—Giotto—and went over to speak to him. He saw the picture. With gentleness and generosity, Cimabue offered to take the boy and train him in the arts. As we know, Giotto became a very great painter, but without Cimabue he could well have lived and died as an unknown keeper of sheep.

How like this is to the story of David! David too was a shepherd lad. David too was *discovered*. By the grace of God David was taken from the sheepfold and placed on the throne. The gentleness of God through all of David's errors made him great.

Whatever of greatness is ours today is the result of God's gentle ministrations to us.

Usually, when we speak of greatness we are speaking of results. The real greatness is the quality that produces the results. Giotto's greatness was not

the pictures which hang in great galleries. His greatness was the skill of his eye and hand, and this skill
he owed to his master. David's greatness was not
the city of Jerusalem and the large kingdom. His
greatness was the quality of leadership which he
owed to the Lord who encouraged him.

The greatness within us, which we feel is at its
best just now, is our likeness to our Master. He was
the greatest among all when he walked this earth,
and yet he was the servant of all.

Would not our greatness lie in the ability we have
to serve others? Is not humility the mark of our
greatness? Why was David chosen from among all
Hebrew shepherd boys? Why were we chosen from
among many?

The secret of greatness, Matt. 23:1-12.

In words: O Lord, I throw myself on thy gentleness.
Through the years thy kindness and mercy have
brought out the greatness in me. AMEN.

50. THE BEST OF EXPLORATION

"Ask, and it shall be given you; seek, and ye shall find; knock, and it shall be opened unto you."

—Matt. 7:7

It has been said of Columbus that he was forced to leave much of his map blank. There was much of the world unexplored, and Columbus had not the time to do it all. Since the days of the great Christopher other voyagers have filled in the map.

There are other unfinished maps: our scientists are trying to fill in the map of outer space; our doctors are trying to fill in the map of health—so many people in our day are busy exploring the unknown! But the greatest of the unfinished maps is that of the spirit.

Jesus gave the invitation to exploration long ago, "Seek, and ye shall find."

The tragedy has been that so many have been content to see the other maps fill in while the spiritual map has remained blank. This worried the apostle Paul. He told the early Christians they should go on in knowledge. He wanted them to be able to take the meat of the faith and not stay with the baby milk diet. "Line upon line, precept upon precept, here a little, there a little."

There is no better time in life than in mature years to engage in this best of exploration. We are aware of the territory, we are excited by the stories of those who have ventured far out, we are equipped. We stand at road's end and view the far mountains.

Best of course is that we know the way. Jesus called himself the way, and he told us that he went to prepare a place for us. He said that where he was going we could follow.

How wonderful if each of us could fill in one small part of the soul's map! How satisfying if someone after us could avoid dangers because we had charted the course!

A great exploration into the land of giants, Num. 13:21-33.

For pilgrims: Father God, may I continue to explore until I find the city that has foundations. The city built by thee. AMEN.

51. THE BEST OF HARVESTS

"He that goeth forth and weepeth, bearing precious seed, shall doubtless come again with rejoicing, bringing his sheaves with him." —Ps. 126:6

"What did he leave to grow?" This is the question that a biographer put to himself when he started the study of a famous person's life.

"What did he leave to grow?" What did he drop by the wayside as he walked through the world? What words did he drop into the minds of men? What deeds did he start? What dreams did he put in young hearts? What ideas did he contribute?

What we leave to grow behind us, and what we leave to grow after we are gone will determine our harvest. We know that the New Testament is quite clear in statement. We have read that we shall sow and reap. And whatever we have sown we shall reap. God does not change the seed. Now is the time to think back on the precious seed which we have sown. For the harvest will be precious, also.

In Colonial times two men came to the New World. One brought to the wilderness a packet of gold and jewels, while the other brought some envelopes of vegetable and fruit seeds. Each sowed what he had brought. The first reaped a harvest of greed, violence, and envy, but the second reaped the life-giving foods that saved a colony.

As we move into the harvest time of life, we shall be glad. The sacrifices for God and man will bear fruit. The tears shed for the sins and misfortunes of the world will water the precious seed. The kind words spoken will come back a hundredfold.

For all the labor, for all the heartbreaks, for all the dark days of the past, we are about to have our harvest. And we may surely trust the Lord of the harvest.

Added knowledge, Gal. 6:1-10.

Seed bearer's prayer: O Lord of my life, thine was the seed I bore. Thou hast promised it will not return void of fruit. I wait with joy. AMEN.

52. THE BEST OF OWNERSHIP

"All things are yours . . . whether . . . the world, or life, or death, or things present, or things to come; all are yours; and ye are Christ's and Christ is God's."

—I Cor. 3:21-23

An aged professor loved violins, and he loved beautiful Oriental rugs. Diamonds brought a sparkle to his eyes as he studied them. This elderly teacher haunted the stores where such valuable things were sold.

But he did not once purchase a violin, a rug, a diamond. To his pupils he said that he owned these things anyway. Why should he bring them home? Since he was at liberty to walk through the places of business and gaze upon the precious things, they were his. Since he was permitted to touch them, to discuss their merits with the merchants—they were his. This is the best kind of ownership.

And this kind comes only with the years. In youth ownership has an exclusive quality. Two little girls —sisters—rushed to meet the postman on the days before Christmas. How many cards had he brought for each of them? Some of the cards would bear both names. The girls called these "both-of-us" cards and cast them aside—they wanted only their very own. So much in God's world is "all-of-us" treasure, and we learn to rejoice that this is true.

Paul was not giving the world to the Corinthians. He was not writing their names on things present and things to come. He was not saying that they and no others belonged to Christ. He was telling them that they had reached the peak of ownership. They were joint owners with all redeemed and dedicated souls. Not only would they share in the things of now, but in the things of yesterday and tomorrow. Their ownership was eternal. There is no poverty for the child of God.

About things, Luke 12:22-31.

God will listen: Eternal Father, in whose hands are the riches of all creation, I thank thee that thou hast made me a child of thy household. AMEN.

53. THE BEST OF SALVATION

"For God sent not his Son into the world to condemn the world; but that the world through him might be saved."   —John 3:17

A man from a foreign land was lecturing in the United States. He was highly educated, well-dressed, suave, personable, self-assured. He thought to bring some humor into his remarks as he said, "You send missionaries to us. They say we must be *saved*. What do they mean—save us from what?" And thinking of his happy circumstances he chuckled. The audience chuckled with him.

Perhaps he had one wrong word; perhaps he might have listened to the missionaries without that word. He was thinking of being saved *from*— John uses the word *through*. The world is saved *through* our Lord. As we take time to ponder on what is the best of salvation, we may profit by thinking after John.

A big-game hunter may use his gun at the right time and save another person *from* death under a lion's claws. But, after thanking him, the saved person might go on his journey and die in the jaws of a tiger. Salvation must be better than that.

By his life and death, the Saviour has become the sieve *through* which must come all things before they reach his beloved. All anguish is experienced by him first. Even death must be tasted by him before it can touch us.

And now that we have experienced this salvation we do not fear the tigers of every day, we do not fear the pain, we do not cringe from bodily changes. All things are through him and can work us no ill.

If only the lecturer had known (as we know) that a person is saved *through*, and *for*, and *to* salvation might have seemed a good thing to him.

Salvation proclaimed, Acts 4:5-12.

And accepted: Heavenly Father, I affirm once more my acceptance of the great salvation to eternal life *through* the Saviour. AMEN.

54. THE BEST AT THE END

"Better is the end of a thing than the beginning thereof."   —Eccl. 7:8

An artist begins a picture. He has a piece of bare, unlovely canvas, and he has a handful of worn brushes; nearby are the messy tubes of colors. Using these materials, he begins to daub on the paint. In one corner he puts some gray, perhaps; in the center he sketches a vague outline of something. The beginning of the picture is discouraging. As it stands, the artist would not think of hanging the canvas in a gallery. And if he did—who would look upon it?

But when the painting is done! How beautiful! How people flock to see it! The end is ever so much better than the beginning. We find the same when we work on a jigsaw puzzle. And our lives are the same, as day by day, year by year, God works upon us.

In the beginning we were of little worth to the kingdom. In the beginning our virtues and abilities were barely formed. In the beginning God seemed to us a harsh taskmaster. But at the end! Now we are beginning to see God's plan worked out to the full. Now the full effect of the colors shows. As the poet said, this is the last "for which the first was made."

There can be no doubt that as long as we live God will add finishing touches. We will not wish that the process might be hastened. We will wait patiently for our completion, and each new addition made by our Creator will be a promise that something magnificent is intended.

Even Jesus said of himself, "I must walk today, and tomorrow; and the third day I shall be perfected."

When God's fruit is ripe it will not fall. It will be plucked gently from the tree of this life, and it will be added to the eternal treasures of the Lord.

Likewise, Prov. 4:14-27.

Pray without ceasing: Take my life, my love, my all, O thou who hast first loved me. My times are in thy hands. The best is yet to be. AMEN.

Index

(*Numbers refer to meditation numbers*)